FACTS ABOUT WATER

To Mary
with affection
and admiration of how carefully
you look at life.

Love—
Sara

The Two Bird
15 NOV. '98

SARA BERKELEY

Facts About
Water

NEW & SELECTED POEMS

NEW ISLAND BOOKS
IRELAND

THISTLEDOWN PRESS
CANADA

BLOODAXE BOOKS

ISBN: 1 85224 292 2   Bloodaxe Books (UK)
        1 874597 04 9   New Island Books (Ireland)
        1 895449 28 6   Thistledown Press (Canada)

First published 1994
in Great Britain by
Bloodaxe Books Ltd,
P.O. Box 1SN,
Newcastle upon Tyne NE99 1SN,

in Ireland by
New Island Books Ltd,
2 Brookside,
Dundrum Road,
Dundrum,
Dublin 14.

in Canada by
Thistledown Press Ltd,
668 East Place,
Saskatoon,
Saskatchewan,
S7J 2Z5.

Bloodaxe Books Ltd acknowledges
the financial assistance of Northern Arts.

Thistledown Press Ltd acknowledges the assistance
of The Canada Council and the Saskatchewan Arts Board.

New Island Books receives financial assistance from
The Arts Council (An Chomhairle Ealaíon).

CANADIAN CATALOGUING IN PUBLICATION DATA
Berkeley, Sara, 1967-

    Facts About Water

    Poems.
    ISBN 1-895449-28-6

I. Title.
PR6052.E57F3 1994 821'.914 C94-920199-5

Cover printing by J. Thomson Colour Printers Ltd, Glasgow.

Printed in Great Britain by
Bell & Bain Limited, Glasgow, Scotland.

For Michael

Acknowledgements

This book includes poems selected from Sara Berkeley's collections *Penn* (1986) and *Home Movie Nights* (1989), both published by Raven Arts Press in Ireland and by Thistledown Press in Canada.

For the new poems in *Facts About Water*, acknowledgements are due to the editors of the following publications in which some of those poems first appeared: *Agenda, New Statesman & Society, Poetry with an Edge* (Bloodaxe Books, new edition, 1993), *Prism, Times Literary Supplement*, and *Wildish Things* (Attic Press, 1989).

Contents

FROM **PENN**
(1986)

Everything green

Seems like this day is winding on and on
shedding things as it goes
down towards night.
Everything green
is pouring out of crevices.
When I go out the heavy boughs
bunch their blossom into tight fists
hailing down the mouth of earth.

I am asking green to heal me
or in some gesture
mutely to acknowledge me,
but the wind is changing colours
back and forth, somehow preserving purity
of green, on the top, and on the underside,
green closing her throat
to my tentative desires.
Am I not worth that one sign?

curious george

it's a long day thursday and curious george looks at it sideways
the sun is hot but the wind blows it all over crazy daisy's field
when winter comes and the sky is bitterly blue
   then flocks of hungry waxwings come back to cirrus bay
curious hungry george is watching cloudbanks happening
in a lonely windfilled sky there are no questions
in winter skies the rain comes when the clouds are hard and smooth
   then curious raindrenched george is quietly glad
all along the ridge on otis mountain
windfilled reeds are whistling and bristling, flattened to the east
shy otis mountain, barebacked in the wind
   curious george's mountain, and he smiles when he hears its name
trees that are quiet in the sunshine
square off a field that belongs to a widowed maid
the rest of the world is wild but the field is sleepy
   and curious sleepy george is still, watching the sky
the long day thursday is nearly ending
and all over pennypies island a thousand island pines
are dressed in many splendid nightblue shadows
   but curious shadowswept george is afraid of their trembling boughs
rain will be long days washing the summersoaked mountains
and later on when ice is dry on the windfed reeds
otis mountain will darkly slumber through sleep in the face of winter
   and curious winterwarm george will be smiling again

Penn

I woke this morning and Penn was there.
With him I walk barefoot on broken glass
and swing sideways from the breeze
spreading the summer dust.

Breakfast with Penn is a shady corner of the day
he watches the floating orange peel, I tell him lies.
Like children do.

Penn gets in his car and drives
and when the dust has settled
it is clear and noon and I am drinking
cold liquid by the pool. Can we
cross the world by Tuesday?
I say it's hot today. Penn thinks so too.
Together, apart, we swallow
tastings of the day. They slip down easily.

And down the strand on Saturdays
the grasses stripe young lovers
(we are not watching
but our eyes burn anyway)
and beach-long waves sift round
stories of heartbreak and of calm.

It is evening. Penn sleeps.
And I become much older
with this late shaking of the leaves.
I have promised I'll die easily. Penn
says I never miss my cue.

Through the gratings of the evening
he gets on his bike and rides,
and in the small, receding shadows of the day
the wheels turn in a loose metal kind of grin.

Out in the storm

This storm explodes while it is still dark.
I have no flight to watch my flight
from here on up – riding, riding my storm.
She blows the sky aside for me to pass
and from her back the ground looks
faraway. Rainswept. Black.

A coiled coastline writhes in a swirl of sea,
lightning spills yellow road across the fields.
She swoops. Riding storms is fun –
she bucks and rears like real horses.
Who is old in her timeless gale?
She blows a tunnel through the years.
Winded words from the doubling trees
as she gallops past. Riding storms is easy!
Gliding on a tide of rain –
oaks are not afraid of rain.

Time to bring her home, my storm
but reining her is hard.
And long after she has bolted to another sky,
below me waits the road, yellow in the silence
and the oaks are never afraid.
Driving storms is fun until they crash.

Brainburst

Sad, tremulous light
stands shyly before intrepid shadow,

the integrity of darkness
hides not but washes me –

I am too bright. It is making me cry out.
Walls topple towards me but never fall,

and red cars
smash green cars

again and again, though I scream a warning
always slow smashing through the pinhole

of a pupil, which will not look away.
Rivets do not swivel. So I rhyme

to comfort: an odd wish
for confidence in metre. I tick,

and soon it is no longer I who am bright,
who cries out.

Revival night

Hard and hot in her room, way down
in the brittle heat, where no birdsong
reaches her, her wordless cries
shock the sleeping night,
names and numbers draw back
and she sees nothing in the paper gloom.

Coiled grief curling her limbs,
she cries out, making the mirrors crack
and water spout, waking the walls,
but still the stubborn earth will not move
or open wide enough for her to fall.
Outside the blowing sand bleeds,
staining the shallows red.

Long after the last ocean drains
she lets a nightdress make her
pure again. Warm and tender
in the healing light, she loses
hours in a rippling sleep,
waking with washed eyes. Searching
behind the crusted lids, she hugs
the morning, her fingers working
funny shadows in the silver light
like small impatient flickings
of a silver knife.

Chrysalis

I find you washed up on your own shore
among the small stones dragged up in reluctant shoals
with the pull and swing of the water still in your veins,
and the brittle shells whispering secrets bright in your inner ear.

It must be close to four by the way the shadows fall and settle.
Should I tap the glass web that shrouds your limbs
to plumb the silence of your coming
or wait by the chrysalis for your soul to emerge
with wet and crumpled wings – a flickering, frightened thing
shedding the hours like loose skins
while you slip dreamlessly through the layers of day
and the wide earth stretches in unbroken song,
yawns a sigh to touch your folded limbs,
keeping the clouds idly at your sleeping fingertips.

At evening when the rain glances off the hours
and the shy friends gather in the dark,
duty bends me smiling to the earth –
your trail blazes nakedly in the open sky,
casting your shadow to drag the deep
where minnows tremble in their quick flight,

yet such a thin slip of life scarcely parts the air
and letting me put my two hands into your side
you still ask across the aching silence:
Now are you full of pride?

In St Etheldreda's

You do that small thing.
Know nothing, think nothing,
where the unlit stone
supports dead prayer of seven centuries
massed in drifts against muted glass.

The slow beat of awakening consciousness
is the one you move to
and climbing, memory on memory,
remain unsure of the presence, three-personed, whole,
which moves to your side after so long,
and doubt, and climb back down.

In St Etheldreda's
the echoes are prolonged
and purple is worn
brushing up against the candle flame

and you have been close as you will ever be
to an admission that the flame,
that same flame, burning,
is causing you pain.

Although you know nothing
and may soon stop wanting
the reassurance of feeling again,
for now, you do that small thing –
understanding nothing, believe all,
and the certainty is awful, reverential, calm.

Unseen

The only blind man in the gallery
is missing Whistler, Braque, Matisse;
tells me not to try the colours out
on such forced memory, but asks instead
that I be part of his absurd joy
on the street, the open street,
because down his mind
he sees the tiny soldiers charging –
it's the Light Brigade –
and somehow
the colours in *Still Life on a Mantelpiece*
begin to fade.
I have no words for such things anyway.

He says the city
is forcing her skull through the flesh of streets,
lays a finger on the pulse of coming trains
(that rumble is the dark grind of suture upon suture)
and long before warm air stirs the jointed stick
he has heard them cry their sweet whistle
along the veins, under his feet
the white bone shivers
into fissures as he steps quickly
in the train to take him home.

Coming to

I wake from some distant place of dread
(is everything spinning sadly out of gear?)
but you lie sleeping and I'm sure you dream
(how fine to build a house without foundations
and coolly scar a treeline with the roof)
coiled shyly about the bed. You are
a brute, lunging, wondering *does he bruise.*
Sleep drags this admission
from your defenceless form,
calling me cousin, sister, wife.

Over at the easel
colours have wrapped themselves on canvas,
fierce in the patterns of our dreams,
a picture two lives deep.

The Judas flower

When the sun purples the low end of the day
he obediently lights the room.
Here is my chance
to stroke his hair
and touch the soft, round collar-ends.
But tonight he is staying very still
to separate the restlessness of limbs
from the fearful, early stirrings
of a sense within; his clear skin
so easily fingerprinted
by the blundering of my hands, and though
I want to ask him for another chance
I say instead it is time to end his play.
His eyes obliquely roam familiar walls,
burning the air in a delicate, suffuse way.

My son already knows
the cord is cut and tied
the liquids of birth
long dried.
He tries in a childish game
to take narrow breaths, restrict
the rise and falling of his chest.
Without looking, I know that
it will stir again, hold out until
the last and then
reach up and out and back
in the ceaseless draw of life –
it's a suffocating, impotent,
leaden-legged flight,
and he lights up the eleventh hour,
my son, my Judas flower.

He drew back always

When he dived in water, the ripples
spread out, out to the ground we stood,
and I suppose we thought
how heavily he breathed when night was down,
how he was the perfect son,
and then
something in him was shot far wide
and they said sometimes you can read the sign
in the pattern of dropped sticks;
tried to make out the fault lay
not in the way he was shaped
but in the way a star warped its orb
long before we thought of love.

And his eyes would say
that air mustn't torture us the same way
when I asked why he hid his face
walking the North Strand on Saturdays.
Whether the fault lay
in air or sound
or in the way
dropped sticks hit the ground
he drew back always
showing the screaming bones
and I had to lead him home.

All this
because a pair of swallows crossed the sun
as he was born
or on the day he was begun.

Song

Yesterday I heard your song of being
no longer dead
you sang to earth three times
and hearing no answer
you sang to me instead,
opening a silent drawer full of good things.

The sharp pain
was folded there among the scarves
and fluttered lightly to the bedroom floor,
let fall unseen
as I became many childish things
before the mirror – Empress, Princess, Queen –
the perfect image came of wanting it,
of course you would allow me vanity
and a little pride.
I was thirteen and three-quarters when you died.

You, in a crisis,
always threw a wide expanse
between you and the nightmare visions
crossing the horizon,
a camel train in a constant desert:
there the narrow tunnels,
there the great heights.
But though you allowed me vanity
and that little pride
you also threw me from my refuge at your side.

Yesterday I sang your song of being
no longer dead.
I sang,
and sang again most loudly in my distress
they were three cries to earth
each without answer
the answer comes from wanting it
and I have never stopped wanting
so I sang to you instead.

Death in a stranger's head

Four years since you
laid your hand on the wicker gate
coming with a half-child's face
as close as you dared,
looking to me for reason
having died in a lover's head somewhere.

And I –
I saw a running light and describing it, said
it is love without beginning or end,
it is the tightest circle round the sun,
and you will thrive in the memory of no one.

But having died in a stranger's head
you were looking for the moist earth,
the silence of burial,
and it was not reason
saying here was a man, coming
unbound to a nub of pain
from a lover's unopened door
nor was it reason
dictating that you should come to me for more
of this troubled shame.

Four years since the night
I slept, while you were torn apart
questioning whether the elements really were
air, fire, water, love, earth.

And when you came wearily to my bed
I felt that you were hot to the bare soles
and later I heard you in your sleep.
You said *no, no*.

Cycling back

A sense of your name fills the place.
He has left his bicycle quietly weeping in the hall
and climbs the stairs: a dead umbrella, dead cigarettes
litter the room where he thinks you are.

A sense of the recent past
spreads its stain on a blank page
where the four white letters of your name
throw stiff shadows across the day.

Your absence sends out feelers along the walls.
He is standing, picture-bright, framed in the door.
You had filled up every space with so much self
that the empty air rusts down in flakes.

Your skin smelt of honey and salt
and he searched for some meaning to your dreams,
sure he could rest in their familiar arms,
but they had the aimlessness of wild things,

and when he reached out to still
the restless, yearning movement of your neck
you recoiled in a tight spring; a shower
of vibrant, blue triangles sent across the room.

He is cycling back to any age,
pedalling blindly, dimly aware
he cycles away from an empty room
where he thought you were.

Oranges

The orange colour fills the veins,
the orange threads the bones.
She glides into the driest of my dreams,
that boat with oranges on the canal
cleaving the water with her orange laden bows
through great June nights. She does not come
in little pieces, she is tidal,
unified and smooth. You lay your hands
on them then – like two round, firm breasts,
the orange glowing in the veins.
No miracle emerges, only
the prickling of skin leaving the flesh
of oranges that slip quietly by the banks
from Fairways where the meadows bob
and the opiate afternoons drip like ice.

Someone has found a church,
someone else has thrown away a stone
as easily cast as chosen, like oranges
with their clamorous colour, with their voice –
wrung from a supermarket trolley –
or picked from the boat where the others
bubble to fill the gaps; and the ear is ripe
for the water-throb of the engines
sensing the barge loom,
hideous in night's gaslight, staid
when morning's feathers settle placidly
to noon, and white milk curdles
with each of the orange drops.

Hejira

Have you left the silent bed
or is a shadow hovering
trapped within a life of girders
and the grey pools
reflecting sins and dimpled with the sleet
on iron, snow-dressed days?

When the sheet is drawn
and you hide, naked, from a bitter reproach,
I am rocked, petals blown.
The world begins by swallowing me whole
and spitting out the yellow aftertaste of grief.
Ghosts already crowd the corners of the room.

They have shorn the fields since then
rising like stubbled jaws
grey-massed, grimacing, and no birds
alighting for the grain.

You will never let warm air play
on your bare arm again.

The parting

1

You lower my emotions, sealed in their casket,
to the sea bed, knowing I have nothing to say,
paring down to presence and absence
the sad abstractions of our last day.
My throat grows heavy between your hands,
my heart gets tossed away.

2

A shadow is working hard against the night,
working furiously on a morning wall
the shadow cast by fifteen beams of light.
I am a child's bright stone
longing to be the weapon of your fight,
I am the fifteen beams coming straight down.

3

In brief moments when a nerve winks out
it seems as though you will always be there.
The heart kicks – and then you are removed.
You are climbing down the angry white stairs,
you are the shadow resting on my skin,
and we, a double splash of oars into the still air.

FROM **HOME MOVIE NIGHTS**
(1989)

Little river

When harm is done
your sorrow
creaks along like an ice-floe,

and then it is no man's remorse
but a hunted animal
tangling in briars and tearing free,
on and wantonly on from the small wrong –
but I can be a river where the scent will drown.

I am the river where you come to fish,
lean and fleet where the line drops lazily in,
trembling with the slight fish just below my skin,

and where the threaded fly
brushes winnowing riverweed
my warm current carries the light twig
and the small wrong

downstream, and above me on the wooden bridge
you swill water in the pail,
ready for all I have to give.

Just don't walk out in front of my bike

Don't walk out in front of me
when I'm pedalling so hard,
quite likely to cycle over some edge,
because I could take you too
or you might unhinge the symmetry
of my beautiful, clear-eyed bike.

You ran me over with your passion for fast cars.
You know, you are
only one of the men I know
and in my own, shy way,
I like them all; you scorched me slightly
with your fire-fascination, but I was right
to be an empty, earthen cruse
when you tried so hard
to fill me up with every liquid that I like,
and when you want to be a wave
come up from the bed all crest and plumage
I've got to do my best
to tip my weight – beaches burst a seam
when you froth shorewards,
and is it for fun you tilt beneath me?

On September mornings there is usually
a slight ice to be broken between us
and in the face of all this
I must request
that you do not walk out in front of my bike.

Scarecrow
(for John)

I danced with a man of straw.
the music blew through his prickly arms,
his heart was a reed –
it went with the wind –
his smile was wry, tinderish to the touch,
there were seeds for teeth,
I could hear the pods cracking
as he lit a song.
We danced for a week, I was danced dry,
I heard the changes being rung in me
and had I been a bird
I, too, would have risen with a shrill, vowel sound.

Death of a red flower

I am not clear today, there's a bloom on me –
you've got gentle hands and I may cry again
for you replenished that unhappy reservoir,
that lake we found, hugging in on itself.
Even our silent awe sent ripples
to the other shore.

You discard things as you understand them.
After ten years you know well
how a whole parcel of your life
may be bound tight and put up on a shelf.
Memory is a red flower,
the best bloom,
chosen by you from a drenching of colour
on a March street-corner.
Today I put it in dying water.
it has lasted these ten years,
only now is it bruising.

Do you?

You came for Sunday afternoon,
you stayed for tea
and look what you left behind –
every memory, sheafed carelessly on my window seat,
of you and someone who looks sadly,
sadly, sadly like me.

I sometimes think I see you
loitering in the shrubbery
without intent, idling nonchalantly
under the weeping beech; I sent
those memories, lovingly enveloped, to that
memorable attic flat,
someday I may even
stand at your door,
hopeful and
completely uncalled for;
but distance is proving such a very thick wall
I can hardly hear you any more.

Do you feel this at all? Do you?

I don't want his name in here

At his death they cried that way –
the sun howled, rain came.
I loved the grief, it had so many parts,
I hugged it to me on cold days
when the air was full
and love took longer
to recall.

His image is burned on my retina.
I get dry-throated whenever I look,
I whistle in the dark,
I haven't a hope.
But light flocks, circling, and dawn brings
soft shapes pacing in an upper room;
maybe it will snow
big, forgetful flakes blunting the grass
and the edge of hurt.
I don't want his name in here
but I don't regret.
I turn the death over on my palm –
it is a small, soulful thing,
it could blow away.

Maker of rain

I hear the muffled voice of my heart,
the fretted moan,
when the day sinks to its knees
all full of cries and heavy skied,
and I know
you still have the power you had
when we slept in the dim room.

When we came in late
full of the labour of sundown
and dropping dark,
drawn close by the doors creaking under our skin,
and the cats brushing, saucer-eyed, against the dark,
how you wove the threads of me
into slumbering cloth.

I answer the voice of coming rain
with words of the sunlogged room
where we lay until late in the afternoon.
You still have that steady hand –
opening my sorrow
wide as it will go.
Maker of rain,
I ghost the intimate room
where you wove the sheen of my most precious moods
and I know
you still have the power you had
when we slept in that dim room.

Launderette

The harbour town is washed with dirty greens.
I hum an old lullaby until it hurts,
and the dim lines of poplar trees
breathe in time to the breaking
and the healing of the sea.

I find the slatted comfort of the wooden seats,
sit facing the machines,
watching them digest their wet, cotton meals,
and through the tumbling heat
his shirts grasp feebly at the glass door,
dancing for me, pleading with me –
so I concentrate
until the helpless linen tells how heavily
his life lies, how he wakes late to feel
the dark come down, obliterate
the comfort of old things, childhood things,
long put away, dust-mantled;

and I try to fold something more
into the warm damp of clean clothes –
something he will come upon,
intent in that unguarded moment
leaning back to catch the second sleeve,
something blue-green,
or all the colours of a child's wish.

A study of us together
(for Niamh)

This is how I go with her:
you can study us together,
we listen to the water notes
that tremble down the ear's tunnel;
we hear
the spring's first impulse to tears
checked by the wind's sigh;
we're both washed away
on the wild silk, moonroll of spring tide,
my sister and I.

The same anvil beaten and beaten
until the shape is white-hot beaten.
You can carry away this fashioned thing
and it is not love
but stuff of the marrow and nerves
and of the blood.

Sometimes we are two notes
a breathspan apart – the breath of a tiny bird
with the hint of a minor tone beneath his heart,
sometimes one is shorter,
we are sometimes both the same,
and how easy to citizen
this world of two notes
with the faintly minor beat of wings
and a brave face put on things.

Sometimes we listen
to ghost notes making the memory tremble
and the room is washed through,
washed free of all trouble, and we
are two small girls again, eating ice cream,
we could be any age,
seven, eight, nine.

Ten

Her tenth birthday
sends an ache from eye to eye.
Across my brow she strings the decade
she has made; down my spine
her lovely fingers let the years course through.
A pool forms at the base.

Double-figured, she unwraps her gifts,
turning up her tiger-lily face, freckled, sure
of a rich capacity to please
and if a sudden impulse should arrest
my empty lap to gather her in,
my shoulders to have her weep at them again,
I wonder could I keep her in the dark
where she would lean only to my sun;
but when she sleeps she seems briefly
to join the dead, taking on
their ice-edged white, not to be
touched in case a flaw
should shoot across the skin.

Even taking her leave for school she takes
too much; I wish her well,
she swallows the wish,
a slim match, eating her flame,
archly blackening,
so I offer her the gift of choice;
she chooses lightly with her delicate hands;
an hour of silence, poppy seeds,
the tale of Ruth, such things.

Allowed out on her own,
she comes in, wind-blown,
arms full of contradictions,
laughter about the eyes
with their mute agreement of grey and green;
she should have been
named for a queen, for she loves
to presume,

she does it with a simple calm, counting
mountain peaks among her natural heights.
These rumours reach me by a side-wind:
I never gave her leave to grow
so leggy-geranium tall.

Once she raised the lid on a box of light;
her face dazzled, and I thought I saw
a child of light – but in a waking dream
she let it close again. Has no one seen
how a little light still
plays about her when she smiles?

Home movie nights

Ratcheted, in stills,
how thin and brown the smooth-limbed
brothers, throwing off their casts of sand
(bury me! I am a dead man!)
framed in loose rolls of celluloid,
and I, smaller even than the buried ones,
up there on our sitting room wall.

I was once caught under a giant wave –
they brought me out alive
(they did not save my life
for I was saved on celluloid)
but through the wave I saw them dive for me.

All my life they brought me, pearl-like,
from the waves, and now, well used
to handling the names of men
long gone from me, and unfamiliar grown,
and opening the letters home
I do most of my
wringing of hands
alone.

Pole-bound

Pole-flown, jittering in the sun,
you can see me for miles:
I am the jubilant one,
highflown; my spirits soar and whip,
knuckles white, I grip the wind.
We are bound. We are all thoroughly bound.

I have all this wasted passion
and how do I sleep?
The restless breezes paw me awake;
my tongue is minced, it ripples uselessly
I am the one who always sees the dawn.
I sleep fitfully.

Rain moulds me, abject,
to the bitter pole;
I brush my eye-lashes wearily against its cheek –
yes, this is reluctant love,
everything's under lock and key
in my heart. Everything's shut down.
I can see for a hundred miles around
but I am bound. We are all closely bound.

A time of drought

I am with you on the long road,
I keep time with your pale and winded
giving in, I don't let go.

Today I shared a day-long lifting of the weight.
We water-skiied at a warm place,
we pitched in, learning the feel.

I saw your shoulders straighten with the load removed,
you held tight to your nerve, riding the surf,
laughing your ropeworn laugh –

I thought you'd rise above the mounting dread,
your child's shrinking from the end of things,
but you were sinking, anchored at the wrists,

head bent to those depths plumbed from an early age.
I watched the water rise against your dry sides,
I saw it suited you to drown,

my heart kicked up enough sand to hide itself
and lie back still, for you scorn places
where the rock-falls make a shallow pool;

you held tight to your fraying nerve,
you took hold of my words, they came
by the roots, as in a time of drought.

Wintering

Of course I feel you gathering up to leave.
In our tightest, briefest arguments
I crush nettles with my blind left hand –
the child in me peers through a grid of fingers,
my eyes are an open wound.

Your lies have piranha teeth,
freshwater white;
the stones of the river grieve
until they are worn smooth,
and pain has its way with me –
a great fish, nosing at my spine.

Because I will not try to blunt
this helpless, piercing sight,
you push me to one side.
The cold air salts my face.
Perhaps this, too, is a cure,
for you are slight
and leave no trace.

My hand digests the slowest nettle juice,
I have no scars to show
but I have heard
the muttered refrain of wintering
tremble up from a flurry of dried leaves
at your heel; it goes
bury me, I shall grow in spring.

Convalescent

There's smoke in the air although it's spring;
people are shedding muddy boots and things,

slamming their private doors
on rooms with sofas and TVs.

I fall into the wind –
it rights me, mildly,

and I walk like a convalescent
down a tree-lined path,

wood-soothed, thinking of bough
and bark and all that will come

of the nutshell, the circles
in the circles the lathe handles

lovingly with its gaze,
the hacked limb a lumberman heals

with his dab of bright paint.
Somewhere friends are waiting,

lies in their hands,
hands by their sides.

The swing

The afternoon's awry, it slivers off in curves.
My dress makes a crimson pendant
at the garden's throat; I swing

causing a frivolous shiver of green
across the lawn; I am cradled there
printing this crescent I wear

across the brilliant, livid-sided air.
All this swinging stirs the blood,
makes whole the filled-up heart,

until the garden, stiff in its joints,
begins to make fluid the swing to good
and the return to wrong –

and when I fall, just let me lie
for the more I try to be featherlight
the heavier I become

and the more I try to be winged
and sleepless, the heavier grow my eyes;
my senses list to the warp of the earth.

Whose voice is this,
singing the swing to rest,
shrouding it in loveliness?

Closed out

I saw you close me out with that one look,
the flick of a smile-edge emptied ash
in a sad flutter down

and I am only some dull creature
thudding softly round, not pretty, though gentle
and so unwitting, treading white snow brown,

bewildered by you
burning through the trees like a whipping wind
silver-witted, while I am slow iron –

and when you opened my hand
and found the first bloom
wincing from a late frost, on the palm,

winter fled through the air in a fine dust,
making me feel I end soon too
now you have closed me out with no word.

Less than a hundred hours

I have put on a warm skin,
I have come in
from the garden, where a pallor is caught
on every thorn.
You know it's you I see at evening
before the light goes.

The secret alters with the hours,
sleep slows the colours,
but in the morning, waking
from some warm place,
it flowers timidly against the covers,
pale on the pillow where six hours of sleep
damp down easily to a drawing of breath.
You know it's you I see at evening
when the light goes.

It is less than a hundred hours
and the secret fits so close
I have almost grown to it,
something I have touched a lot,
I know its shape by every light
its colours deepen as the day arches
towards noon, dragging its heavy form,
by night it has become
hot and damp in the palm, and now
it is less than a hundred hours
until you come.
You know it is you I see at evening
before the light goes.

The figures in the rain

Over all the flowers I hold
you have sometime bent your head, inhaled
my peony's bluff soul
my violent rose.
And every time your train goes
my life lies fallow about the tracks
like bramble whips
the small blind winds blow dark without you
I try opening colours to wander through
but you so briefly visit everything I own,
sing to me of the meek figures in the rain,
then leave with the scent of my scarlet blooms
still colouring you. Sing me the song again
of the meek figures
for there is often rain,
tell me the story of the figures of doubt
then bend your head and depart,
leaving me to wring from my heart how
if I had come from the dark,
if I had only looked up
from the dark crook of my arm
life could have been so warm
and I could have seen so much.

The hung man

I have hung, spider-kicking
between laughter and fine sorrow
when this happens I drink coffee and I
don't know what to do.

From the top of the world
every slope runs down.
I'd hate to die right now –
I have this scent between skin and bone,
it smells of a nightmare town
that knows no primary colour.

You have no idea what it's like
to hang with hope and a fear of falling,
it is strange and strong
how the thoughts run
where limbs won't go;
I am taking the winter sun
on the backs of my hands,
pleased I am not of the dead ones,
I am safer now than I have ever been
but sometimes you just feel
unclean.

The courage gatherer

With the sun too close
a loose wind catches me off guard,
dreams flock to my skirts
and cling there like a litter
I'd steal sleep to feed.

Asked exactly how I feel
I answer from the fields
and summer lanes
where I have come
gathering courage.

A wing shadow strobes the lane;
from time to time the future sinks
with the black doubt of people
leaving me – but hope comes out
in her lovely shimmer, her hair behind,

untied, fresh on the morning,
never fully woken, never still.
I follow with my arms
full of the songs she leaves,
all of the same brave tune.

FACTS ABOUT WATER
(1994)

Man in balloon

He was what he was,
he dreamed it was more.
Some said his spirit kindled at his throat.
He stamped it out.
He kept his emotions at bay. One day
finding them wrung, he weighted and drowned them
one by one. Pity sank without trace,
fear sank, then love. Setting his face,
he held his great anger down
and saw it drown.

He felt so empty then. The reservoir was low,
the ducts were dry, the blood was cold.
He could not find his feet, his head was light,
like an air balloon –
he clambered aboard
and rose.
Bottomless the sky; looking down
he saw the cloth of the earth unfold,
the pattern of river and town,
snake of a track, quilt of cloud.
When would the secret be told?

All day it was light, the night
kept him afloat. At dawn
he felt wings. He knew flight.
He soared.

The drowning

He took his stones
down to the pier at dawn. The waves were in
from Japan, a few ships lingered,
the city sighed and turned, the sky
crept up from the sea.

He dropped a line and waited for fish to bite
his nails throbbed, the hairs of his head
pulsed at their roots
his blood pushed to be let out.

The sun rose
he thought of the many ways with a smile,
for the weight of a stone he went down
slow as a feather's fall
razor shells brushed his wrists
small fish kissed at last his willing lips
he blushed,
brushed a pier support with heavy hips,
shoals flashed overhead
close to the old world.

He lay still
the seaweed clung to his brow
gulls swooped for his bright rings
up in the hills
hawks hung in the warm air
and dreamed of his eyes.

The church was full.
The first sod on shiny wood
fell with a thud. Inside, cold and dry,
he laughed till he cried.
The last shoe turned in the dirt,
and God, all angry and hurt,
turned on his heel,
left him his weathered dark,
his first taste of earth,
his drowned thoughts.

After the story broke

After the story broke
he sat in the window
watching the skinny girls hugging themselves
and the sleek cars slow at the curb.
He picked up his pen.
'I miss my favourite girl,' he wrote;
he put the pen down. It was there
the story broke.

It was dark
in the narrow alley of his life,
she had been light,
he was silhouetted in her light,
a man with his hopes
all riding the same high wire.
As long as she was there
he held to the burning train of his dreams
as though there were time
for every hope to bloom
among the cobblestones.

After the story was borrowed and blown
he walked with his head down,
he stood in the dim-lit alley
listening for trains,
trying for the face of his girl
but he could only recall
how she struck light
and his shadow was thrown
long, like one
who stoops to a heavy load
and looks suddenly old.

Man in flight

Sometimes he was like
a powerful bird.
His climb into air,

his struggle to master the air.
He would fight with what
was not really there,

he would beat wings that were
mere arms.
He would sink to his knees on the bough,

he would listen to wind until
the wind was right.
I loved the jubilant arc that described

his flight.

Facts about water

Be ready for the flood, they said.
I gathered my skirts. No flood came.
Beware the danger that comes with a man,
they said. I waited for the fall.
In blinding light
he stumbled to us from the stones.
Was this the man? He fell at our feet,
fire, famine, flood.
Give him his name, they said.
I was drawn to the man, I told him
this is your name, and then he was all I saw,
the first I knew of endless, immeasurable calm,
the whole struggle over and done.
I had expected pain, instead
he treated me with care, folding and wrapping,
I had never been given before.
He gave me to myself, said without saying
love if you will, but be warned,
I have very little.

Here was a man without the anchor of dreams.
He blinked in the sun, he hardly seemed
at home in his set of bones.
I felt his uncontrol
reined in with a shaky hand. I said,
if you need me in the night call out.
Trains run beneath my house.
His flame flickered, but did not go out,
I conjured a green field to steady him,
no gate, no way in or out,
but a cool mile of young grass
and four spare dry stone walls
to hold him in.
I had never held anyone in before.

In return, he brought me to his shore,
he wrote in the sand
facts about water.

Minim, fathom, barrel, cord,
magnum, gallon, jeroboam.
He said, when you wake far out,
dream a boat, and with these things
make good your return, and he wrote:
sextant, compass, dipstick, dial,
plumb, octant, nautical mile.

He left me sleeping,
I woke without fear,
in a rigged vessel, sails and mast,
I dreamed my way to dry land,
acre, arpent, section, square,
league, light-year, township, air.

Zoo Gardens, Berlin

My watch has stopped,
the heart you gave me is broken.

In the zoo gardens
gas lamps glimmer in the first rain,

slow figures pull their dark coats closer.
By the bridge the puddles are slate grey,

rain hisses gently on the river,
the sounds stay close to the water.

In their enclosure
the animals skitter and bleat,

they don't appreciate
autumn's melancholic hunger,

the ongoing tug of the rain,
they are hungry or tired or in pain.

I am not any of these things,
my name is shallow and no pools form

I wait for a while at the rail,
I lean down and my coat falls open,

the animals do not seem
touched by anything, but I hear

the watchtick heart in your mouth
telling of wet leaves

and the black weather to come,
the colours of air.

Potsdamer Platz, Berlin

The corners of the world moved close
after the wall
fell and was flattened and filled,
people dared to walk
in the wide streets and the empty places.

Potsdamer, where an old man stumbled to a seat
in the weeds, Potsdamer Platz where they will
build and lose a world.

Point by point a shape emerges,
the blocky offices, flawless, linear,
behind the old memorial church with its
bombed spire
that I admire because it
fails to please,
because it hangs out human memory
in the breeze,
because it grieves.
Clean glass heals the open stone,
the markets drip jewellery,
silver bands and candles, hats,

and over Spandauerstrasse
the statues standing out against the dusk
sing of the wide streets and empty places,
of Potsdamer Platz where they will build,
two years after the wall
fell and was lifted and filled,
with hardly a scar, the tar tissue knitted so well,
I stand for the last time in a place
wide as the space a man's life takes to fill.

Paddington

The taxis line up in the sooty air,
I wait for a later train.
Above us all a net is cast in the gloom

it hangs above the clocks you can hardly see
for grime. They have given up the struggle,
they wander in time as the platforms thicken

and grow lean.
I wish I were not this faint dishevelled me
with the stoppable heart, always an eye out

for the leap of light,
the shaft of yellow I turn from,
healed for a spell. The sun is red,

the ordinary lives
are running out on narrow rails,
the engine growls at the rear, I stop my ears,

I turn from the snub end of the beast,
ashamed that the sound
can so dismantle my peace of mind.

I look to the three arches for black grace,
a sense of light coming apart
and coming together, up in the birdnote rafters

the organ-music heights; I think
I have to climb down, get on a train,
sit tight.

Fall

(U.C. Berkeley 1989)

We sit over Indian bones
and over the silent, sitting up, buried ones.
Bob Hass laughs about Dickinson
and tells us it is
okay to be slow,
and confusion
is all part of what is meant to be.

I finger the silence
that follows a poem's end.
It is the sound
of having been there, the hard despair
that follows pain getting words
and after rain you can hear the drops
staying in the trees.

Sometimes the day tumbles early
but coming up from the Mining Circle
the grass yearns down to the figure of a girl
in bronze, green as rain, and such bewilderment
is part of what is meant to be.

Poles

The mind runs north to south
the weirs in the river of thought turn round
the rivers in the heart's valley turn;

heading west
I lose my sense of self,
of home, and how the land lies.

The bus groans as though in pain against
livid barriers; prevailing winds
fold their gags into my mouth,
the land lies north to south

her waters turn to follow the moon,
the cold lies flat along the ground,
frosts calm the earth's trouble,
she is black and white from pole to pole,
the great whites, north and south,
the snow wastes and ice caps,
and then the deeper blacks

where space roars, way beyond,
as though out there
all darkness found a voice.

Famine

I am the dog they ring bells for.
Emptier than ever, hollower,
and I am not hungry, or
hungry. I have lost hunger.

My space contracts,
I always escaped before.
Down at the shore
the sand is running out.

Infinite hunger
yearns at the rim of the world,
famine gnaws my bones.
Hunger is the core

beneath the film of mist
and the comfort of men; their raw god,
the one they ring bells for.

Airport

We split seconds as the engines climbed
to drown the time. On tiled floors
your bags no longer looked like yours
and distance telescoped,
the giddy surface was too sheer for us.

To keep a footing on the rolling earth
I played a game
of missing you ahead of time,
you played this too,
I heard you turning over in your mind
shots of the things you left, brought to light,
developed in the red room behind your eyes.

The wheels began to scream
there wasn't enough oxygen
I saw you lean in to the heavy swell
and hope to swim
across the tarmac to the white machine
and flounder in.

Reflex

She crouched in the corner of her head
the ache of sanity passed
the bricks of the wall held her there,
eyes quenched,
darkness about the mouth
her back to the words.

She was a crafter
moulding her absence with bare hands,
dovetailing silences,
learning and learning, blind and divining
the age of shadows, their grainy touch,
the lie of them.

We brought her shelter,
a cardigan of words she would seldom wear;
the nouns she devoured,
survival balanced, melting, on the tongue;
but the verbs, tensed in their paradigms,
she had no purpose for,
and cast away.

Mist

The singing goes on, lonely, in the mist
long after dark. Up on my second floor
I follow the score.
On the window face
a clammy smile, spreading, white,
nothing behind the eyes,
the chilled limbs invading my few rooms.
I turn to find at home,
comfortable in my easy chair,
body without bone,
whispering with the books,
sweating the air, exchanging looks
with the family photographs,
billowing secrets under its breath.
The kitchen cradles the dark,
the fridge has started quietly to hum
to my foggy guest, the phone
shrilly
fails to ring. If it would only rain
and damp down my unwelcome friend,
or I could make the move to fire,
and paint my home
with flame.

Loom

Our house stands
quite alone on the road
it darkens and darkens,
the doorbell rings in the gloom
we cannot let light in,
we are seldom home.

The house is many-cornered
it has an angular voice
its spirit is noosed;
light from the streets
makes frosted squares on wallpaper there
the drive lights make more squares;
shadowy paintings, blurred books
jigsaw the dark,
these pieces make memory up.

We are kept tight within our bones
by places, names, and childhood happenings,
meals that have been taken there,
people wearing faces they will cast away,
sun shining through the rooms,
getting lost somehow.
No need to shape the tones,
the house spins its own,
that frail loom the builders raised in days,
they put the wires in
that hum and sing in spinning out
the crazy, half-heard tunes
that make the spaces at my fingertips
vibrate, as though sent
through a different element.

A letter

Down to cold stone
to whet my heart. It is not long,

the letter with the burning lines.
Hearts are sore, mine sings

a mournful tune
I have to listen to. The beach is raw,

white waves crashing down on sin,
sky washed and the water in,

coke can in the undertow,
a gull runs shakily at the edge.

Wave after wave
and the foam climbing up the dark

underbelly. The dark could punish
but it comes too late – gull takes fright.

A tightness climbs my throat
my wings are trembling,

white envelope,
the end, the wrapper, the crumbs, the dregs.

The weekend falls back like a medium weight.
The letter walls me out, I feel

nothing
and nothing is better.

Uncle

All day his name
has reached the satellite, come down,
and clear along the line, my brother says
that he dropped heavy in a room of light,
heart caught on the last beat,
a round stone in the deepest lake
from the dizziest height.

The story tells
of two men working in the fields
of women threshing grain
how does it go? That one will stay –
the grain lie lonely in the palm
and the chaff be blown.

All day long my uncle drops,
the ripples open out.
He has mislaid the place where words wait.
There must be another
alphabet
known wherever there is sun.
I long to speak that simply.

Tightrope

Beneath the taut rope
your arms go up in a shudder of sparks,
your fireworks light my act,

you are ready to catch.
But my fall is feather-downed,
limbs weigh little in this dream

I live the whole descent through its blurred veil
it makes me a Catherine wheel,
a quick storm in a dry time.

Something leads me safely
down the cool tunnel of the fall
bone-dry and skeletal

I touch stone on both sides,
you spread the nets below
and I realise

that before I flew was a dark time –
I might have been some huddled animal
digging and blind; cold head,

fogged heart that would never clear,
never drink the sun –
and I land in a gauze of tears.

Sea-borne

I smell sea-salt from my thoughts
I begin to be obviously
sea-borne, as you were
once dragged from the water's womb,
slimy, sea-green, wreathed with foam,
wearing the weeds of birth.

At your beginning
trees bent, used to one wind,
you gave them another, sent
it teasing from leaf to leaf,
such early greens,
yours was a clean breeze

I took it long before the offered hand,
it blew warm; later on,
hope against hope, I leaned full into it
and you suffered me to change
as the light when an object turns.

You knew by the shy red stealing to my skin
that I had opened flood-gates
and would let the ocean in;
you keep a wind always to my back,
and though my heart is in my mouth,
silence is by far the harder cry.

Fault

I was not built for
the dull rumble of the valley air,
the great steel birds
that fly with a dark grey
whine, grazing the sky.
They fly low in the blue face of it,
they spell out its naked state,
the clouds are at bay.
The fault sniggers beneath the highway,
she cracks her knuckles publicly
but keeps apart her joy,
narrow and deep; some day
she will send a flame
from the scorched well of the earth
and burn off the teeming human layer,
she will burst her corset of rock
and take the air,
she was not meant
for the brittle rib-cage of the bay.

Valley

Wherever you look
she answers back.
You know her by the jewels
set shallow and close
for eyes that narrow
and are never shrewd.
You know her by the good bones,
the many thoughts that fall on gold,
her friends are few
or they hide; her smile is broad
while out of the bullets of fast cars
she invents a war,
under their hail of horns
only such surface gestures can be made,
the nod, the solemn wave.
When there is cause to celebrate
her laughter is canned,
a cast of hawks falls on her parade.
I know her for a young girl,
virginal, pure,
you skin your knuckles
trying to knock some love from her.

Slender girls

Into the risky waters of another month,
bottle and paddle, milk-crate raft,
the children shout from the beach
but she goes against the small choppy waves,
salt in her wounds.

Beyond the shelf the waters make her body
yellow green, and there is no bed,
she wears a fluid dress,
she's a thing of grace now, a girl
from a family of slender girls,

she'll swim like this
on the last day in the first sea,
exulting in
the sweet milk of being alone in it,
and when the water calls
for a change of element,
she'll breathe it in

and that
will be easily done.

At the rails

Life stretches far, many things come right,
the sea yawns crisply to the ship's stern.
Tonight I am possessed
by reaches dark and out of sight,
my hidden wishes race us out of port,
heads high, sailorcapped,
they cheer briefly as we wheel, and clap
against the pier one final time
as the land pencils to a foreign line.
The wind chokes, fouled in the spume,
there are wind-spirits out tonight
our trail is knuckle-white
hard bone under little flesh.
I will wake in waves, wondering
was this where I drowned last night?

The waking

The sudden waking, golden-quick,
describes my spirit as a trick of light,
plays him sitting by my bed,

surprise breaks with simple joy
over my temples, still warm with sleep,
over my cheeks

and down, down to the end of the dark.
Opened from a dream
I am surfacing, but how should I speak?

Brimful, I unfurl a bright sail,
the alphabet sends letters out,
great consonants to fill the sheet,

my head, my heart, my memory
all have warm places for his hands,
I am the bearer of a chalice of calm

I wish him to drink from,
for I have grown to him, sleeping
with his lashes lying at half-moon,

pillowed in wellbeing;
and if I am frightened of change,
of being left behind,

I wrap the similar sounds of words
about the barely wounded bed
and I rock to the warm vowels

whispering brave lists
the alphabet sends,
and I never mind,

for I have grown to him, sleeping
with his lashes lying at half-moon,
pillowed in wellbeing.

Heartbreak hour

His flat is all
oasis, warmth of books,
he gives me tea
and offers the missing piece
of a picture:
low skies and a lake iced-over,
I tell him about
love's quavering note,
he says there will always be
a man's hand cupping my chin,
look to the light, he says,
all ice is thin.

Leaving there at four, heartbreak hour,
the air is freezing over
and the blind animals
fretting in the small of my heart
are begging me
to write the stories of ice and fire,
the journal of leaving behind
oases, and facing
the solid grey door
and my own walls, my silences.

The road to the interior

I thought I would drive
to the end of the sky
to the land's end.

The day was naked blue
the air pearl yellow
all colours were fast

I gunned into the afternoon
as though it were my last
the fear lay sideways on my heart

I got so thin
the bones shivered beneath my dress
I held a prayer between tongue and cheek
– I used to believe
– I used to believe
everywhere stones rolled over their holes
blotting out sound

the car thumped on the dirt track
and swung to a halt
I longed for the sun on wet grass

an end to this dust, from which
nothing would rise up,
my head rested on the wheel

and in my dream
friends came forward to take my hands
but I looked too hard to see them.

Sung through fire

I put a match to music
up came this soft drum
those plaintive flames
those strings.

Fire came down upon my house
many things were lost,
the sun came down.
My children, playing with water,
did not burn.
My father
toying with words
could turn a phrase to burn my ears
but chose instead
love's gentle word.

When I was a child, I fell asleep
to my mother's song
to the light under the door
the muffled mysteries of the adult world.
Sometimes I recall that song
I am almost child again
and to my children
sing lullabies through fire
watching their faces in the red light.

Most of knowing
is not knowing but a guess,
rage at the signs of nothingness,
fury and fear,
disappointment, disillusionment

and in the end
among the ashes
love.

Wasp

This
is the box she's in
full of light and weight
of certain temperature
she has never been in this
particular box
before.
She sleeps to see how it is
to wake, and at such moments
of real fear
as occur, she whispers
earth, wind, water, fire
as though to stay in touch
with the things that are.
But by noon the sun
splits heads
the halves yawn
and roll;
later darkness comes
and then a deeper deafness
this is the time
a dying wasp will ache to give its sting
the box is dark, the dark
heart breaking; she will find light
if she can get out
before her skin stripes
yellow and black
wings petrify.

Patience

A game of patience
the cards tap on the flat
tabletop; it is late,

I keep my letters tucked
down between the flower pot
and night; marry the gentleman
you met in the gallery, they say,
live like we do, be happy,
and write back without delay.

I shuffle the cards,
life is not dealt straight,
the King has left his Queen –
he poured the fire that lit her crown
and when he left she let herself go out.
She sat down.

Memory pulls on its chains,
I find a place
near the end, my wishes are weightless,
I lay the cards
on the rough tabletop, they stir dust,
the motes set up a thin cry.

Her kingdom in flames
by her red King the Queen is laid,
heart, heart, diamond, spade.

In his room

Inside his room, life was
a balancing of weights
it was a memorable sight –
all that man,
contained,
and those who called him mad
trawled that word from their shallow hearts,
yet, spine-arched, their napes too
were resting lightly on the truth.

I first saw him as I swam upstream
he burned bridges
his face took the river colours
he was one who lived perpetual spring,
when he turned after rain,
when he let the leaves be blown,
that was unknowing,
and I too lost time, growing with him,
became a changeless thing.

Like smoked-out rabbits,
ears back,
we fled the turns
of tide, of season, of the day;
and could I have known
that so much fright would fall upon the warren,
on the riverside
and on his spring,
I might have found the perfect height
and flung my spirit down.

He isn't there

She is a single note of the song
without him; she gets it wrong,
the blood stops going to her head,
she sees stars.

She almost gets run over
without him; into rush-hour's cars
she steps out, thinking of
his forearm's blond hairs,
his slenderness.

Everything has a ghost
every spirit has a double
her lost half cries out for its
lost other. She senses trouble
at the source, tries to block out
the wrong sounds, the noise, the noise,
was that his quiet voice? She opens her mouth

but without him no sound comes out.
She stands in the traffic
crying in cold air her single note
and he isn't there.

Burying the elephant

What a grave it took to dig,
burying the elephant,
his shadow lengthened and grew dark,
his shadow rolled over and was gone.
O shock of the spirit when
great things go down.

He was caught in the sun's net,
the sun brought him crashing down,
elephant spirit meeting the ground;
blue eyes muddied with a failure to rise,
earth's yawn must bury him now.

The elephant was heavy-blooded,
stone full, slow with time;
we all came to bury him,
our blue eyes lit with ivory
and a kind of grief;

I had my own pit dug,
feet up, my animal kicked
with stiff limbs; in my hide
my shadow rolled on the grass and groaned,
my spirit grew dark and gave;
elephant trumpet bellowed in the trees,
the forest sank to its knees,
the forest rose and swayed.

What a grave it took
to bury my animal's meat.
I turned his spirit out and now
the darkness is complete.

Man chopping wood

Man chopping wood
looks up to see
the helmeted boys go over,
he can hardly believe –
men in their khaki fatigues, running hard
across the no-man's-land of his back yard.

The whistles are screaming,
he drops his axe; the wood smells
warm, sweet, as it should;
the men going over
throw up their arms as they did
on the old news reels,
just as he had always pictured
Great Uncle John
who was lost on the Somme.

He thought it was all
black and white in the war,
all hands on hearts, flags in the breeze,
he's never seen men sink to their knees
he's never seen them torn limb from limb
he was just
getting the woodpile in.
His wife's in the kitchen, baking pies,
his kid's on the green
playing football with the neighbours' kids,
he tries to scream
but his voice won't come
and quick as they came, they're gone,
it's quiet again,
smell of new wood and raw air
and no knowing if history was played
or statistics made, if pain was real
or death hard
in the no-man's-land of his back yard.

Undertow

I was not gently led
into that inner room.
From where I lay, it always
seemed another room away,
and feeling the wall for a door
I felt the cries of all those girls before
being drawn, drowned,
promised and offered and led
to the very core, and whether willing
or in dread, all
swooping low and following
the flow and irresistable tide
knowing the undertow
was where they always died,
abandoning
every distinguishing sign,
mole, tilt and curl,
number and name,
until they were all
the same and it fell
cold as a cave in the room,
they stood holding the spent flame,
wanting to put it down,
bury it now it was done
and move with the ease of girls
who know themselves,
into a different room.

Once their sound
turned down, my hands
began to burn
from holding memory's hand.
I laid them flat on the cool sheet
and turned my other cheek,
lying easy in a white bed, wondering
when would I be given up
for dead.

A week left

It is clean inside my head,
there's been a storm; things leap there,
up the salmon-falls the sun leaps,
the brightness,
the good feel of the day.
A moth goes fluttering
into the blue candle of the past;
for miles both ways
the road is the same; the houses,
the gates; only the people change.

Back in my room the belongings squat,
soon they will huddle, sad and packed away.
My fists grow small.
There's a week left.
I want to think only of good times –
I am sixteen and tanned
and my fringe is too long;
I am thirteen and playing kid,
the round heart of sunlight
is almost at my fingertips,
the house opens like a flower,
doors are flung wide;
or I am nine and in a new dress,
it ripples and creases dark and light,
but there's a week left,
and I feel stones inside.

I will open my eyes wide,
I will open my ears, I will try
to call some colour to my smile;
the days form a ring,
they have numbers pinned to their backs
the weight is doubling them,
their grim dance shakes me from limb to limb
there are seven of them.

Everyone's cold

He woke in the dark, blind, still inside
the close nature he would like to
kick off in the grass and walk from.
Sun came up, but he never saw.
He was trying to fathom the time
by the depth of his fear
he felt it was light on the street
why was it so heavy in here?

He got up, pulled the shutters across.
The wind looked dull against the thick glass.
He rode the bus to her house
storm tide sucked his heart dry
and flooded it full,
the extra sounds kicked in, the tightness came,
he reached for her throat, to him this violence felt
like love turned backwards,
he waited for time to begin
for sun to blow the earth out,
for cracks to show.
'Everyone's cold!' he cried, but she reminded him
of love, the circle and fall,
and what she said
she said so simply that it broke him down,
he spread till he was
thin on the ground
his snakeskin spirit dreamed in the grass
the quiet went deep, she made him promise
to let go his anger at last
and bury his fear in sleep.

After the fact

Then I lay down.
The train moved and I was trying
not to fall back frightened.
Westminster rose cold between the trees;
I waited for Battersea, the satisfying way
the four white towers would hold me still,
a pillar at either shoulder,
a pillar at either heel.

When the desert arose,
that cup of mine began to thirst for rain.
I lay between two juniper trees
and when the trouble came,
it was quick as steel,
I loosed myself to meet it.

Down England's spine towards the tail
of Brighton, dogs on the sand, Lowry people
arm in Sunday arm along the pier.
There is a way
to grow into my life, to pass a hand
over the damaged face without unreasonable fear.
I walk the planks, beyond the candy floss and beer.
It is all sea to the end of the sea
from here.

Evidence

They came to the end of them,
nettles took hold, the roof fell,
thistles grew right down their hall;
she listened to his doubtful thoughts,
gathering evidence.

Into other people's homes
he made his solitary way,
left his bones in their cold stone jars,
put his hot cheek to their flagstone floors,
heard only echoes there.

She lay under a mountain ash
keeping count of the seconds that passed;
with her free hand she traced a root,
circled and circled the heavy doubt,
cut his name in the dark.

Didn't he see the end of time
chasing minutes across the face?
The heavy cast of early June
fell too smartly on her pain,
would she ever be safe?

She lay counting them to a close,
in her vessel was bitter blood,
truth flooded her deepest canals,
truth found its own level,
close to the bone.

The evidence bore down,
her heart felt the gavel's rap;
where he laid her she didn't sleep,
the silent jury kept her awake,
she would never be safe.

She turned on her side, he knelt in his dark,
kissing the life from her every joint;
she counted elephants, one to ten,
he said her name a final time,
it was over then.

The man I knew

He climbed on his life,
hands ragged, winter-blown eyes;
space revolved around his world,
a million lights were lost in thought –
it wasn't the dark that mattered.

The man I knew
threw his life in the water;
the man I knew surfaced and gasped,
he was survivor, kicking the boards
of the boardwalk, grabbing the rails
for a long haul
back to the real world.

His colours came through.
In his single room
no one held him as he wept
and he was glad of no one.

Without sight, he was
ready for life; kicked dust at the stars,
swung with a measure of hope,
made no bones of it.

All that winter
his letters fluttered to my letterbox;
although I broke the hold, I turned aside,
and read them all, and cried.

On goes
the hungry scissors up our paper lives.
The whole splits, the halves
roll back alone. High on his life
something else, different and good,
can begin. Across his sky
a million lights go on,
his palm ghosts the back of my neck,
his memories reach out and back,
he is travelling light.

Blue Tuesday

Near the end of blue Tuesday
he wrote himself a note
about how miserable he felt;
put on clean socks, laced his boots,
went out to face the weather.

He sat on his step in the sun
until the fog rolled in;
fat fog rolls sat on the hills
and blew across his road.
He went inside, turned the wind down
and knelt by his life, blowing for a spark.

When it grew dark,
he crouched in the dark, fiddling with the dials
listening to the voices fade in and out
spreading the weather.
But news on the hour increased the interference,
the hair on his neck rose
he turned from the news through a snatch of songs,
liquorice tunes he once whistled to.
He rocked and rocked in his white board house
head in his knees, casting around for himself.

It came unexpectedly, like the truth
right at the end, a silence that stilled his hand,
he passed through every station on earth
and in the end, face down, head first,
the hissing silence held him.